Country Ch

By

Norman Goodland

Good luck Ann!

Cover photograph: Pat Sillence

Norman L. Goodland

Published by Paul Cave Publications Ltd.,
74 Bedford Place, Southampton

Printed by Brown and Son (Ringwood) Ltd.

'Sylvia'

Published May, 1987
Reprinted July, 1989

ISBN 0-86146-058-8

CONTENTS

Page

Norman in pensive mood.

COUNTRY CHARACTERS

Country 'characters' — we're not all that different — really. It's just that — like you — our surrounds have made us as we are.

It is true that we are slow to change. But this has little to do with *unwillingness.* It's just that, generally — but not always — we are the last to receive the impact of change.

And this has been so, with our language. The language in which these verses are written. The language used — and I used it, too — in and around the home of my foster-father, Frank West. He lived in the North Hampshire village of Baughurst. It was heard on the lips of his son, Leonard, and is still often used by his grandson, Alwyn, who lives in that area to-day.

It is a language worth remembering. It is not difficult. Its basis was Elizabethan English. On the lips of the characters in this book, you will see how its syntax and grammar remained intact, right up until it died away as common speech, within my lifetime.

To get into the way of it, I lead-in with a simplified version of each of the country characters portrayed, on the left-hand page. You have only to glance across to the right-hand page to enjoy the full flavour of this old Wessex tongue, matching the simplified version.

The old language retained many words of singular rural beauty. There is a small glossary of some of these at the back of the book. And because of its beauty, it was ideal for *composing* verses about country characters and of the countryside.

For that is what I did. Reared in boyhood by Frank and Harriet West, I spoke and thought in the old language, and still can. I did not compose these verses in *modern* English and then translate them; rather the other way round.

Maybe I should not have done that. Maybe I should have left it all to stand on its own. As for that, I must leave you to judge . . .

My foster-father inherited from his father the duties of Parish Clerk, Sexton and Grave-digger to the Church of St. Stephen. He was also Captain of the Bells. He was a water-diviner and land measurer, but thatching was his trade. He died in the 1940s.

You will find him in and around "My Old Chap" (the old affectionate term for 'Father'), "My Missus be a-brass cleanun", "Why do the birds zing, Feyther?", "Prayer for rain", and in "When zun d' dip be'ind Church spoire". Also in the "looking-back" verse, "Let's gwo up to Troaks, Jim", but above all in "You'd like to thatch your roof Zur?"

Both his daughter Muriel and Bill Hussey, her husband, of Ashford Hill, have passed away. When the family went through Billy's affairs, they found a scrawled, unfinished attempt at poetising his feelings for his wife who died before him. I did my best to complete the job in "Billy's Choice".

Sylvia, my wife, you will find in "My wife d' zee things in the sky" and "I d' luv 'ee".

We have fourteen grandchildren — so far — and three daughters and three sons. The wag of the family is in "Guckoo be come", and the most mischievous in "Oh Jimmy-Bwoy" and "The Poltergeist". They all come to tea in "Christmas be come".

We keep an eye on members of the families belonging to us both, surviving from those who have gone before. You will find them in the "'Ogweed b' the geate" and "When Christmas passed this way".

A lovely old lady lives close to me and while she was able, never missed Church for as long as I can remember. She is in "Ellen Sims".

An old patient of a psychiatric hospital where I once worked is in "Up bezide the pig-pens". I used to watch him through one of the upper ward windows, as he worked on the hospital farm.

"Here's to the old hurdle-bumper" contains the advice of the hurdle-maker who used to come every seventh year to the copse alongside us — now a tangled, outgrown jungle with hazel wands topping 20ft high.

"Neil the Ploughman" was a well-known county Champion — and still is.

"Jes — I didn't knaw Jes 'd passed awaay" — was a remarkable habituee of my local, the Malt House. That toast he gave still linked us with feudal times. He knew a few more which sadly I neglected to record.

"The Poacher" — family and friends are still about in the village, so I have not named him. His protagonist was Charlie Pike, the Keeper; the rivalry between them which kept the village agog, now for ever settled in the shadow of the Church Tower.

The artist — you'll find him in "The Hevil Eye". The last man to maintain ridge, furrow, main and drawn in the now vanished water-meadows — only a dim, slow-moving shadow from my early childhood memories, is recalled in "The Drowner". And I am again down on the Hampshire Test leaning on the bridge at dusk, in "Timsbury Bridge".

Judy, my old black bitch of indeterminate lineage, but who turned out to be like a perfect Black Labrador in miniature, behaved like one, and lived to 16½ years, is in "Zummer be come".

And me? In a few observations, "Thunder d' growl", "The Rollerman", "Dids't zee the Lapwing runnen' round?" Thinking perhaps more deeply in "I thank 'ee Lard" and in "Who lives in Farmer Tom's old house?" A little insecure as the years advance in "When the wind d' blaw"; previous to marriage in "I be feared" and also, I hasten to add; *previous* to marriage in "Land Army Gals!"

Perhaps I appear most accurately as I was — and remain! — in "Resolutions". And since these are always made — and broken — in January, which can be bitterly cold, it is followed with "I'll split the log".

I have included a "straight" called "Romsey Abbey". I don't quite know why; except that the Abbey has stood for centuries in the centre of our rural world of "Country Characters", and is likely to do so for centuries to come. A sort of symbol of permanence and security among all the changes.

The "Tailpiece" is clearly not original. I added it because, like all the other verses I have written, it actually did happen.

Norman Goodland

Norman amongst his books — (Photograph: Radio Times).

NEW YEAR

RESOLUTIONS

I'll get one o' they *diaries* —
  like I did once afore!
I'll mark-in times as folks was born —
  an' wed. An' dead. What's more —
the times to get their presents
  an' post 'em on their way!
Then *this* year — not a one of 'em
  'll be missed — on the day!

There's *jobs* as I must see about!
  I'll work me way on through —
an' put 'em down! The seasonal work
  as earns a bob or two —
an' outdoor jobs. I'll make a list
  to stick to every day!
Then I shan't sit about and smoke —
  an' dream the time away!

I'll get up like I always did —
  half after six or so!
Hail, rain or fine, I'll get on out
  an' round the lane I'll go —
an' march along an' come back spry
  as ever I used to be!
An' if my dear wife's still in bed —
  she shall 'ave a cup of tea!

I'll shout those boys up earlier!
  No quarrels then! No 'aste!
Nor breakfasts missed — nor things mislaid —
  no cause for to be late!
An' when they're gone, we'll sit us down
  an' 'ave ourselves a chat —
about them things we *both* want done —
  an' which *first* — to be at!

We'll think about the garden!
  We'll make us out a Plan!
There's time yet to get started —
  I'll dig as soon as I can!
I'll plant those shallots *early!*
  Next month the seed I'll buy!
An' get those broad beans sprouted
  to miss the Summer fly!

I *will* cut-down on baccy. P'raps
  a pipe morn, noon an' night!
I won't go down the Malt House

NEW YEAR

RESOLUTIONS

I'll get one o' they *diary*-books —
  like I did oncest avore!
I'll mark-in times as volks was barn.
  An' wed. An' deid. What's more —
the times t' git their presents
  an' pwost 'em on their waay!
Then this year — not nar one on 'em
  'll be missed — on the daay!

Them *jobs* I got t' zee about!
  I'll scratch me way on droo —
an put 'em down! The zeaz'n'l work
  as earns a bob or two!
An' *outzide* jobs — I'll meake a list
  t' bide by, every daay!
Then I shain't zet about n' smoake —
  'n dream the toime awaay!

I'll get-up like I allus did —
  hafe arter zix 'r zwo!
Caddled 'r voine, I'll mush-on out —
  an' roun' the leane I'll gwo —
an 'tober-on, an' come back spry
  as arn I used t' be!
An ef'n Missus a-bed d' bide —
  she shall hae a cup o' tea!

I'll holler-up they bwoys on toime!
  Nwo hasslen' then — nwo 'aste —
n'r breakfasts missed — n'r things misled —
  nwo cause vor t' be leate!
An' when they'm gone — we'll zet us down
  an' 'ave ourselves a chat —
about they things us *bwoth* wants done —
  an' which vust t' be at!

We'll cogitate on gaard'n!
  We'll meake us out a Plan!
Ther's toime yet t' get at it —
  I'll dig as soon as can!
I'll zet they shallots *early!*
  Next month the zeed I'll buy!
'n get they broad-beans chimpen-
  swo's they dun't ketch the vly!

I *ull* cut-down on baccer. P'raps
  a pipe marn, noon, 'n night!
I 'un't gwo awver Malt 'ouse

midday. Well — p'raps I might
take 'alf a bitter. Or a pint.
Well — *never* more 'n two!
Then 'stead o' nodding in the chair
I'll *work* — the whole day through!

And then at night, come after tea —
we'll 'ave *another* list!
Of things wants doin' round the 'ouse —
so's *nothing* won't be missed!
No gawpin' at the Telly
an' stayin' up so late!
We'll be abed by *ten o'clock!*
Well — *eleven* — at any rate!

What's *that?* 'Tweren't *Missus* — were it?
Hi'm juggered! Be that *snow* . . . ?
Well — I haven't *got* to start today —
tomorrow — p'raps I'll go!
"All right! All right! I *heard* ye!"
What's she just been an' said
Gone *nine o'clock!* God love us!
"OF *COURSE* I'M OUT O' BED!"

JANUARY

I'LL SPLIT THE LOG

I'll split the log!
Bide you indoor!
Wind do cut cruel
down across Moor!

Pigeon be *frozen!*
No bird do sound . . .
Frost bites like iron
deep in the ground!

Deadwood tumbles . . .
Trees moans, an' cracks!
Hazel-wands rattle —
Click-clack! Click-clack!

Wood do split *brittle!*
'Case it d' fly —
I'll watch! Don't worry —
none will come nigh!

I'll split the log —
bide you indoor!
Wind d' cut *cruel*
down across Moor!

midday. Waal — *p'raps* I might
teake a hafe-bitter. 'R a point.
Waal — *never* more 'n two!
Then steid o' noddin' in the chair —
I'll *work* — the whole day through!

And then — at night, come arter tea
we'll hae *another* list —
o' things wants doen' round the house —
swo's *nothen* wun't be missed!
Nwo gawpen at the Telly —
an' stayen' up swo leate!
We'll be abed by *ten o'clock!*
Wall — *eleven* — at any reate!

Wha's *that?* 'Twarn't *Missus* — were it?
Hi'm juggered! Be that *snaw* . . . ?
Waal — it ain't *urged* t' start t'daay —
Tomorrow I met gwo . . .
"All right — all right! I *yeard* ye!"
Wha's she jes ben an' zed —
gone *nine o'clock!* Gawd lumme!
"'O *COURSE* I'M OUT O' BED!"

I'LL SPLIT THE LOG

I'll split the log!
Bide you in door!
Wind d' cut cruel
down acrost Moor!

Pidjun be *starved!*
Nwo bird d' zound . . .
Frost bites like iron
deep in the ground!

Deadwood d' tumble . . .
Trees mwoans, an' cracks!
With-wands rattles —
Click-clack! Click-clack!

Wood d' split *brittle!*
I'll watch un vly!
Dunnot thee worry —
narn wun't come nigh!

I'll split the log —
bide you indoor!
Wind d' cut *cruel*
down acrost Moor!

COURTING

I BE FEARED

When she's due home along the lane —
  I do harken for 'er feet.
If I do look, then she do smile —
  but I be feared — to speak!

My old fool tongue wun't let I!
  It don't know *what* t' say!
I just bides — puzzle-'eaded —
  whiles she do walk away!

'Twould *'appen,* p'raps — if she'd speak *first* —
  of if she'd stop awhile!
But she just keeps on going —
  and all she does — is smile!

I'll tell thee what — tomorrow —
  I'll linger-on in lane —
and if she comes strollin' up 'ere —
  well then — I'll try again!

I'll say, "What's on then, Mary?"
  And not gawp down at feet!
I'll say, "You comin' *my* way?"
  — if I bain't *feared* to *speak!*

TIMSBURY BRIDGE

How still . . . !

All in the river — downside-up —
I see the poplar-tree.
An' weed comes creepin' in the dark
to tangle, where I be.
An' all the mead is wreathed in mist —
as creeps an' twists —
an' lifts — an' drifts . . .

And moorhen 'tchecks' —
an' 'tchecks' again, to tell that she
do know full-well — just where I be . . .

No 'tchecking' now. Down there . . .
somewhere . . .
she's *watching* me . . .

How still!

I BE FEARED

When she'm due whoam along the leane —
  I d' 'arken vor 'er veet.
If I d' luk — then she d' smoile —
  but I be feared — t' speak!

My wold fule tongue wun't let I!
  It dun' knaw *what* d' zaay!
I bides on — buzzle-'eaded —
  whoiles she d' walk awaay!

'T'd ackle p'raps — if she'd speak vust —
  of ef'n she stopped awhoile!
But she jes' kips a-toberin' on —
  an' all she does — is smoile!

I tell thee what — tomorrow —
  I'll mush about in leane —
an ef'n she draws-on up yere —
  wall then — I'll try agean!

I'll zay "Wha's on then, Mary?"
  An not gawp down at veet!
I'll zay, "Bes't comen *my* waay?"
  — ef'n I bean't *feared*- t' *speak!*

TIMSBURY BRIDGE

How still . . . !

All in the river — downzid-up —
I d' zee the poplar-tree.
An' weed d' crope-down in the dark
t' tangle, where I be.
An' all the mead be wraithed wi' mist
as creeps an' twists —
an' lifts — an' drifts . . .

An' waterhen d' 'tchek'.
An' 'tcheks' agean, t' tell that she
d' knaw full-well, jes where I be . . .

Nwo 'tcheckin' 'now! Down there . . .
somewhere . . .
she'm *watchen* me . . .

How still!

LAND ARMY GIRLS

Cawd love-a-duck
the sights we see!
They gals as works along wi' we —
when sun do shine
an' fly's about —
they takes their clo'es off
clout by clout!
And black as gypsies they all be!
They bain't the gal for likes o' me!

Old Bill do look
that sour and say
"They ought t' chase they gals away!
In fellers' 'eads
ther' is no knowin'
what *thoughts* there be — instead o' hoein'!"
But *Martha* — she
do work away —
an' keeps *respectable* — all day!

So draws I up
alongside she —
an' me an' Martha — there we be . . .
She don't look up
'cept now an' then:
an *I* says noth'n. I pretend
as singling-out
is all I see.
But *Martha* — she's alongside me!

Says Bill — "If they gals falls in shame —
they only got *theirselves* — to blame!
But *Martha* — she's
the *quiet* one!
You bide along wi' *she* — my son!"
. . . An' that I will —
for down the lane —
my *Martha* —

she bain't quite the *same!*

LAND ARMY GALS

Cawd luv-a-duck —
the zights we d'zee!
They gals as works along wi' we —
when zun d' shoine
an' vly's about —
th' teakes their *clo'es* off
clout b' clout!
An *blaack* as diddicoies they be!
They bean't the gal vor loikes o' *me!*

Owd Bill d' luk
that zour 'n zaay:
"They ott t' chease they gals awaay!
In vellers' 'eids
ther' is no knowin'
what *thotts* there be — insteid o' hoein'!
But *Marty* —
she d' work awaay —
an' keeps *respectable* — all daay!"

So draws I up
'long-zide o' she —
an' me an' Marty — ther' we be . . .
She dun' luk-up
'cept now an' then:
an' *I* sez noth'n. I d' tend
as zinglen-out
is all I d' zee —
but *Marty* — she's 'long-zide o' me!

Zayz Bill, "If they gals valls in sheame —
they on'y got *theirselves* — t' bleame!
But *Marty* —
she's the *quiet*-un!
You bide along wi' she — my son!"
. . . An' that I *'ull* —
vor down the leane —
my *Marty* —
she bean't quite the *seame!*

MARRIAGE

MY WIFE D' SEE THINGS IN THE SKY

My wife d' see things in thy sky.
She d' see folks a-passin' by;
houses, 'n trees, 'n seas an' things —
an' fat old dames wi' writhin' limbs!

I cain't see nothing!
No — not I!

"Look John!" she d' say, "put down thy prong!
Come up by plum-tree here-along!
Up over top of Eldon look —
cans't see that Shepherd — wi' 'is crook?

I goes on diggin' . . .
"'Ave 'e gone?"

"Come *here* John! I can see 'im plain —
that Shepherd! *There* 'e is again —
with tags and two-tooths, yews and lambs —
and can't you see that great black ram?

"It looks to *I,"* I says,
"like rain!"

"Look John — a stable! Can't you see
a *horse* — a-top that walnut tree?
Where the old ploughman's ploughed 'is lands
beyond the stubble! *There* he stands!

"I cain't see *nothing*
No — not me!"

My wife do see things in the sky.
I *likes* to please 'er. I do *try*
to see they trees an' seas an' things —
an' palaces, an' queens an' kings —

But I sees *nothing!*
No —
not I!

MY WIFE D' ZEE THINGS IN THE SKY

My wife d' zee things in the sky.
She d' zee *volks* a-passen' by!
Houses, 'n trees, 'n seaz an' things —
an' vat wold deames wi' writhen' limbs!

  I cain't zee nuthen!
  Nwo — not I!

"Look John!" she d' zay, "put down thy prong!
Come up by plum-tree yere-along!
Up awver top of Eldon luk —
cans't zee thic Shepherd, wi' 'is crook?"

  I gwoes on diggen . . .
  "'Ave 'er gone?"

"Come *yer* John! I can zee un pleane —
thic Shepherd! *Ther'* 'e is agean —
wi' rags an' tutuths, yaws an' lambs —
an' cassn't zee thic gert black ram?"

  "D' luk t' *I*," I zays,
  "like rain!"

"Luk John — a stable! Cassn't zee
a *hoss* — a-top thic walnut tree?
Where th 'owd ploughman's meade 'is lands
athirt the stubble — *ther'* 'e stands!"

  "I cain't zee *nuth'n!*
  Nwo — not me!"

My wife d' zee things in the sky.
I *likes* t' plaze 'er. I d' *try*
t' see they trees an' seaz an' things —
an' palaces, an' queens — an' kings —

  but I zees *nuthen!*
  Nwo —
    not I!

MY MISSUS BE A-BRASS CLEANIN'

My Missus be a-brass cleanin'!
  I d' say "Let 'er be!
Whiles she d' go a-cleanin' —
  she bain't a-chivvyen me!"

When Master took to tractor
  and poor old Flower were gone —
he d' say "Carter — 'ere's her brasses —
  you take 'em down-along!"

My Missus took an' hung 'em up
  'long-side o' fireplace.
Then — she did start a-cleanin' —
  wi' rags, an' pots o' paste!

Hemmed if that didn't do summat!
  We got brass everywhere!
There's vases in the window —
  where th' old oak walls was bare —

there's saucepans all a-gleamin'
  an' pots an' candlesticks —
and Father's great old stand-lamp
  got *bulbs* — instead o' *wicks!*

She bought a three-legged coalbin:
  a Gran'fer clock as goes —
an' stuck en up in corner —
  an' he d' look nice, thee's know!

So draws I up my wooden chair —
  lights I my baccy-pipe —
whiles Missus goes a-cleanin' —
  an' that do suit me right!

I *knows* 't've cost a *fortune* —
  but I do say, "Let be!
Whiles she's a-cleanin' brasses —
  she ba'int a-chivvyin' me!"

MY MISSUS BE A-BRASS CLEANUN

My Missus be a-brass cleanun.
  I d' zay "Let un be!
Whoiles she d' gwo a-cleanun
  she bean't a-chivvyen' me!"

When Maister tuk t' tractor
  an' poor owd Vlower were gone —
'e d' zay "Carter — yere's 'er brasses —
  thee teake 'em down-along!"

My Missus tuk an' 'ung 'em up
  'long-zide o' voir-pleace.
Then — she did start a-cleanun —
  wi' rags, an' pots o' paste!

Hemmed if that dedn't do zummat!
  We got brass everywhere!
There's vazes in the winder —
  where the' owd oak walls was bare

there's sosspens all a-gleamen'
  an' pots an' candlesticks —
an' Feyther's gert wold stand-lamp
  got *bulbs* — insteid o' *wicks!*

She bott a dree-lagged coalbin:
  a Granfer clocks as gwoes —
an' stuck en up in carner —
  an 'e d' luk *nice,* thee's knaw!

So draws I up my wooden chair —
  lights I my baccy-pipe —
whoiles Missus gwoes a-cleanun —
  an' that d' suit I right!

I *knaws* 't've cost a *fartune* —
  but I d' zay, "Let be!
Whoiles she'm a-cleanun brasses —
  she bean't a-chivvyen me!"

I DO LOVE THEE!

I *do* love thee, Tom —
   don't argiffy, no more!
Thee get thy milking-coat put on —
   an' get off out-o'-door!

The Master's looking out —
   the cows be stood by gate —
don't bid 'ere carrying-on at I —
   't'won't do to be *too* late!

When you come in to tea —
   I'll have it all put right!
Be a good man now Tom, 'cause I
   don't want no rows tonight!

Master be lookin' *ard!*
   He'll wonder where you be!
You 'urry-on afore 'e comes
   a-bellowin' for thee!

Yes — I d' love thee, Tom —
   don't argiffy no more!
Here — get this milking-coat put on
   an' get off out-o'-door!

THE ROLLERMAN

I seen 'er turn, a-watchin' I!
I seen 'er rise as I comes nigh!
Three eggs set down
there on the ground . . .
Swing-out there, Captain —
out! On by!

Off she do go! Up she do fly!
'Phwit-wit! Phee-oo-whit!' I 'ear 'er cry!
All white and black . . .
Come thee on back!
I ain't a-touched 'em girl —
not *I!*

Pull-out there, Captain! Now she stoops by —
stands there a-lookin' — wi' one black eye!
Danger is done —
in she do run!
Spread theeself *down,* bird!
Don't mind *I!*

I DO LOVE THEE!

I *do* luv 'ee Tom —
  dun argivvy, nwo more!
Thee get thy milken-cwoat put on
  an' get off out-o'-door!

The Maister's luken out —
  the cows be stood b' geate —
dun bide 'ere carr'n-on at I —
  't'unt do t' be *too* leate!

When you comes in to tea —
  I'll 'ave it all put right!
Be a good man now Tom, 'cause I
  dun' want nwo rows t'night!

Maister be luken *'ard!*
  'E'll wunner where you be!
You 'urry-on avore 'e comes
  a-belleren' vor thee!

Yes — I d' luv 'ee, Tom —
  dun' argivvy nwo more!
Yer — get thic milken-cwoat put on
  an' get off out-o'-door!

THE ROLLERMAN

I zid 'er turn, a-watchen' I!
I zeez 'er rise as I comes nigh —
dree aggs zet down
ther' on the ground . . .
Swing-out ther', Captain —
out! On *by!*

Off she d' gwo! Up she d' vly!
'Phwit-wit! Phee-oo-whit!' I year 'er cry!
All white and black . . .
Coom thee on baack!
I ain't a-touched 'em gel —
not *I!*

Wook-off ther', Captain! She d' stoop by —
bides a bit — luken — wi' one black eye!
Danger is done —
in she d' run!
Spread thesen *down,* bird!
Dun't mind *I!*

MISCHIEF

WHY DO THE BIRDS SING, FATHER?

"Why do the birds sing, Father?
  Why do the pigeon 'croo'?"
"They'm *speakin'* to each other.
  They *talks* — like me an' you!"
"Do you know what they'm sayin', Dad?"
  "Well, son — sometimes I do!

"That wych-elm is a giant look —
  all silvered in the sun.
They pigeon loged-up in 'is 'ead
  spin *thoughts* — to puzzle un!
And down along the copses
  where barley-field do run

"the birds is all opinionin' —
  'ow nice and warm the day!
'Ow nice o' breeze as tips the leaves.
  t' blow they clouds away!
If you bides still and listens —
  you can *hear* what they do say!

"That artful robin tinkles —
  that blue-tit rings 'is bell —
they thrushes, and they blackbirds
  joins in quiet-like as well.
But — 'cause she knows they'm jealous
  the little nightingale

"do wait her turn politely
  to agree wi' one and all;
but that old jay do drowned 'er —
  wi' an 'arsh and quarrelsome call!
And rooks slings cuss-words at 'er —
  they don't care for 'er at all!

"*That's* why the birds sings, nipper —
  they *talks* — like me an' you!
They'm *speakin'* to each other —
  that's why the pigeons croo!
And you can 'ear what they do say —
  if *you* bain't talkin', too!"

WHY DO THE BIRDS ZING, FEYTHER?

"Why do the birds zing, Feyther?
  Why do the pidjun croo?"
"They'm *speakin'* to each other.
  They *talks* — like me an you!"
"Do you know what they'm sayen, Dad?"
  "Well, son — zometimes I do!

"That wych-elm is a *giant* luk —
  all zilvered in the zun.
They pidjun lodged-up in 'is heid
  spin *thotts* — t' puzzle un!
An' down along the coppices
  where barley-vield d' run

"the birds is all opinionin' —
  'ow nice an' waarm the daay!
'Ow nice o' breeze as tips the leaves —
  to blaw they clouds awaay!
If you bides still and *lissens* —
  you can yere what they d' zay!

"That artful robin tinkles —
  that blue-tit rings 'is bell —
they thrushes, an' they blackbirds
  jines in *quiet-like* as well.
But — 'cause she knaws they'm *jealous*
  the little nightingale

"do wait 'er turn politely
  to agree wi' one-an'-all;
but that wold jay d' drowned 'er —
  wi' an 'arsh an' quorlsome call!
An' rooks slings *cuss-words* at 'er —
  they dun't care vor 'er at all!

"*That's* why the birds zings, nipper —
  they *talks* — like me an' you!
They'm *speakin'* to each other —
  that's why the pidjuns croo!
And you can 'ear what they d' zay —
  if *you* bean't talken, too!"

OH JIMMY-BOY

Oh Jimmy-boy, my Jimmy-boy —
he do sit down on stair to cry!
I don't know why!

Oh Jimmy-boy, what can it be?
'ave School-marm been goin'-on at thee?
You won't tell?

You got your shirt-tail inside-out!
Do big lads pull at thee about —
when you runs by?

Oh Jimmy-boy, my Jimmy-boy —
'twon't do no good to bide and cry!
Now — thee tell I!

Here — I do know why you do squinney!
'Tis 'cause thee hasn't got nar penny!
Don't pipe your eye —

You take one boy — and run-off quick —
old Jes don't shut 'til pretty-near six
if you do fly!

Well I'll be hemmed! There he do go
a-grinnin' an' a-laughin' so
as he runs by!

Oh Jimmy-boy, my Jimmy-boy —
when he do sit on stair to cry —
I *do* know why!

OH JIMMY-BOY

Oh Jimmy-bwoy, my Jimmy-bwoy —
he d'zet down on stair to cry!
  I dun't knaw why!

Oh Jimmy-bwoy, what can it be?
'Ave School-marm been a-gwine at thee?
  Wun't tell I?

You got yer shirt-tail inzid-out!
Do big lads pull at thee about
  when you runs by?

Oh Jimmy-bwoy, my Jimmy-bwoy —
'twun't do no good t' bide and cry!
  Now — thee *tell* I!

Yer — I d' know why thee does't squinney!
'Tis 'cause thee hassn't got nar *penny!*
  Dun' pipe thee eye —

You teake un bwoy — an' run-off quick —
ole Jes dun't shut 't'l prett'-near six
  if you d' vly!

Well I'll be hemmed! Ther' 'e d' gwo
a-grinnen' an' a-laughen' swo
  as he runs by!

Oh Jimmy-bwoy, my Jimmy-bwoy —
when he d' zet on stair t' cry —
  I *do* knaw why!

THE POLTERGEIST

Ah! Just the feller, Jimmy-boy!
I *wanted* to see thee!
You ever 'eard o' 'poltergeist'?
You don't know what it be?
Well — he's a little *Spirit* —
as 'ave come to live with we!

He's nothing to be *feared* of —
but you would be surprised
at the places he do get to —
an' fiddles, pokes an' pries —
an' the mischief he do get at
for a Spirit of 'is size!

When Mother pumped the Primus —
what's think! It wouldn't go!
That there *poltergeist* 'ad been there!
The little so-and-so —
'e turned the washer inside-out,
then screwed un back, you know!

And when I switched my lamp on
to rack the cows at night —
the *battery* was upside-down
an' put back awkward-like!
An 'cause o' that there poltergeist —
I couldn't get a light!

He dropped suds in wi' golfish
to try and keep 'em clean!
'E stuck a pencil through the soap —
all *sorts* of things I've seen
where 'is igglin', jigglin', twiddlin'
interferin' *fingers* been!

But never I do *see* 'im!
'E's as cunnin' as can be!
So in the end I thought I ought
to 'ave a word with *thee!*
Because I'm sure my Jimmy-boy
is *just* as sharp as he!

So if so be you *see* 'im —
don't *jump* at 'im — nor shout —
but come and let your *Father* know
as *poltergeist's* about!
'Cause if I can catch 'im at it —
then — Jimmy-boy — LOOK OUT!

THE POLTERGEIST

Ah! Jes' the veller, Jimmy-bwoy!
I *wanted* t' zee thee!
You ever 'eard o' 'poltergeist'?
You dunno what un be?
Well — 'e's a little *Sperrit* —
as 've come to live wi' we!

E's nothen t' be *feared* on —
but you would be surprised
at the pleaces 'e d' get to —
an' fiddles, pwokes an' pries —
an' the mischief 'e d' get at
for a Sperrit ov 'is size!

When Mother pumped the Primus —
wha's think — 'er 'ouldn't gwo!
That there *poltergeist* 'd ben there!
the little swo-an'-swo —
'e turned the washer outzid-in,
then screwed un back, thee's knaw!

An' when I switched my lamp on
to rack the cows at night —
the *battery* was downzid-up
an' put back aukurd-like!
An 'cause o' that there poltergeist —
Hi couldn't get nar light!

'E dropped suds in wi' gwolfish
t' try an' keep 'em clean!
'E stuck a pencil through the soap —
all *manners* o' things I zeen
where 'is igglen, jigglen, twiddlen
interferen' *vingers* been!

But never do I *zee* 'un!
'E's as cunnen as can be!
Swo in the end I thott I ott
to 'ave a word wi' *thee!*
'Cause I'm hemmed-sure my Jimmy-bwoy
is *jes* as sharp as he!

Swo if so be you *seez* un —
dun't *jump* at un, nor shout —
but come an' let yer *Feyther* knaw
as *poltergeist's* about!
'Cause if I can catch un at it —
then — Jimmy-bwoy — LUK OUT!

CUCKOO BE COME!

Cuckoo be come!
Wake, Missus — wake!
There he do cry
right on the date
April the first!
Well — *he* ain't late!
But *I* be, you!
Wake, Missus — wake!
  Hear Cuckoo!

Where be it, boy?
Oh — you can see?
Let I come in then —
up on that tree?
That bain't no cuckoo!
That *pigeon* be!
Cuckoo bain't *grey* —
nor d' sit like *he!*
  Tain't *cuckoo!*

You knows it is?
You heard him shout?
Well — I wouldn't *swear* to it
I must get out!
I'm going-on down —
get Mother out!
Lord — I cain't bide
this husslin' about!
  "Cuckoo!"

Up across mangold-ground
I'll go on through —
cuckoo still sits there —
a real *grey* one, too!
Boy says 'tis *cuckoo?*
Why — that bain't true!
He be a *pigeon!*
He do say 'Croo' —
  not 'Cuckoo!'

Boys up at window
wavin' at me!
Laughin' 'e is!
What's-up wi' he?
'Cuckoo!' he d' go —
dang 'e — *I* see!
First day of *April!*
He've a-caught me!
  'Cuckoo' *I* be!

GUCKOO BE COME!

Guckoo be come!
Weake, Missus — weake!
Ther' 'e d' cry
right on the date
April the vust!
Well — *he* ain't leate!
But *I* be, you!
Weake, Missus — weake!
  Year guckoo!

Where be un, bwoy?
Oh — you can zee?
Let I come in then —
up on thic tree?
That bean't nar guckoo!
That *pidjun* be!
Guckoo bean't *grey* —
nor d' zet like *he!*
  Tain't *guckoo!*

You knaws 'tis?
You yeard un shout?
Well — I 'ouldn't *swear* to 't
I must get out!
I'm gwine on down —
git Mother out!
Lord — I cain't bide
this hasslen about!
  "Cuckoo!"

Up athirt mangold-ground
I'll gwo on droo —
Guckoo still sets there —
a real *grey*-un, too!
Bwoy says 'tis *guckoo?*
Why — that bean't true!
He be a *pidjun!*
He d' zay 'Croo!' —
  not 'Cuckoo!'

Bwoys up at winder
wavin' at me!
Laughen' 'e is!
Wha's-on wi' 'e?
'Cuckoo!' 'e d' gwo —
dang 'e — I d'zee!
Vust day ov *April!*
'E've a-*caught* me!
  'Guckoo' *I* be!

HIGH SUMMER

SUMMER BE GONE

Summer be come.
Weather be fine.
Grass'opper sings in blaze.
Barley be dry —
wheat-heads milky —
ripples on oats do race.

Daisy d' stare.
Bindweed d' flower —
butterfly dances, look!
Dogrose be out.
Thistle d' seed.
Foxglove be stood by brook.

Nettles is tall —
poppy do droop.
Bittersweet flowers 'angs down.
Pimpernel eyes
brick-red d' show.
Old dog to pant — and frown!

Here — Judy-girl!
Out o' this heat!
'Tis sent-down too strong for thee!
Come to the shade
under the weed!
Stay in the cool — wi me!

ZUMMER BE GONE

Zummer be come.
Weather be voine.
Grass'opper zings in blaaze.
Barley be dry —
wheat-heads milky —
ripples on wutts d' reace.

Daisy d' stare.
Bindweed d' blaw —
buttervly dances, luk!
Dogrose be out.
Thestle d' zeed.
Foxglove be stood b' brook.

Nettles is tall —
poppy d' weep.
Bittersweet vlowers 'angs down.
Pimpernel eyes
all reddled d' shaw.
Old dog d' pant, an' frown!

Yere — Judy-gal!
Out o' thic heat!
'Tis zent-down too 'ard vor thee!
Coom-you in sheade
unner the weed!
Bide yere in cool — wi' me!

THUNDER DO GROWL!

Thunder do growl!
Where do un stood?
All black an' lowerin'
there — in the wood!

Sky do brass o'er —
old sun d' glare!
Skylark bides on
a-singin' up there!

Down d' fall lark!
Out d' go sun!
Birds is all *quiet* —
all except one!

Storm-cock do sit
high on that tree!
Shoutin' at thunder!
— Bain't feared o' *he!*

Thunderclouds tower!
Raindrops do race —
Storm-cock bides hollerin'
back in 'is face!

Thunder draws on
over the hill!
Storm-cock bides jaunty.
Singin' there — still!

THUNDER DO GROWL!

Thunder do growl!
Where do un stood?
All black an' low'ren
ther' — in the wood!

Sky do brass o'er —
owd zun d' glare!
Skylark bides on
a-zingin' up there!

Down d' vall lark!
Out d' gwo zun!
Birds is all *quiet* —
all except one!

Storm-cock d' zet
high on thic tree!
Shouten at thunder!
— Bean't feared o' *he!*

Thunder draws tall!
Raindrops do reace —
Storm-cock bides holleren'
back in 'is feace!

Thunder skulks off
awver the hill!
Storm-cock bides janty.
Zingin there — still!

THE POACHER

I sees 'im in the beech-grove
as stands atop the hill!
The *Keeper* there a-lookin'!
Bide *quiet!* And bide *still!*

I sees 'im on the *stile* there!
But one thing I *cain't* see —
I cain't see my old *lurcher!*
I wonders where he be?

Nightjar 'ave stopped a-whirrin'!
That blackbird — he do shout!
That Keeper — 'e *knows* something . . .
'Ow 'e do 'ang about!

Where *is* that blessed lurcher?
I'll give 't to he, I will!
Why dang! 'E's right *be'ind* me!
Bide *quiet,* boy!
  Bide *still!*

THE POACHER

I zeez un the beech-grove
as stands a-top the hill!
The *Keeper* ther' a-luken!
Bide *quiet!* An' bide *still!*

I zeez un on the *stile* there!
But one thing I *cain't* zee —
I caissn't zee my *lurcher!*
I wunners where un be?

Night-jar 've stopped a-whirren!
That blackbird — *'e* d' shout!
That Keeper — 'e *knaws* zummat . . .
'Ow 'e do 'ang about!

Where *is* that blessed lurcher?
I'll gie 't to 'e, I will!
Why dang! 'E's right *be'ind* me!
Bide *quiet,* bwoy!
  Bide *still!*

THANKSGIVING

ELLEN SIMS

At Church on Sunday mornin's
we'm done-up in our best —
the women wi' great 'ats on
an' fair-to-middlin' dressed —
all easin' this way an' across —
an' squintin' at the rest!
  But Ellen Sims do come in *black* —
  an' she do wear a *little* 'at —
  an' she do sit-down — at the back.

When prayers come sort o' longish —
wi' elbows on me knees —
I wonders what's for dinner.
I thinks about me bees.
I 'ears the sparrows quarrelin'
up there inside the eaves.
  But Ellen Sims *right down* do bend.
  Nor sits back up on seat agen
  'til we've all said the last 'Amen'!

When parson's in 'is pulpit
an' 'e do bummle-on
bout things as I cain't understand
and folks as dead — an' gone —
'owever *short* 'is sermon be —
to me, 'tis terr'ble *long!*
  But Ellen Sims do sit like wood
  as if she's 'earin' somethin' good!
  An' sits there still — when we'm all stood!

An' when 'tis all got over,
we 'angs about outside
whiles womefolk to chatter.
And there we 'as to bide
'til they can yarn wi' Squire's wife,
or Parson comes long-side!
  But Ellen Sims do pass between —
  that *quiet* — she bain't 'ardly seen . . .
  An *some* — don't even known she's *been!*

ELLEN SIMS

At Church on Zunday marnens
we'm done-up in our best —
the wimmen wi' gert 'ats on
an' fair-t'-middlen' dressed —
all easen' thic-waays an' athirt —
an' *squiggen'* at the rest!
   But Ellen Sims d' come in *black* —
   an' she d' wear a *little* 'at —
   an' she d' zet-down — at the back.

When prayers comes sart o' longish —
wi' elbows on me knees —
I wunners what's for dinner.
I thinks about me bees.
I years the spadgers quorlen
up ther' inzide th' eaves.
   But Ellen Sims *right down* d' bend.
   N'r zets back up on seat agean
   't'll we've all said the last 'Amen'!

When parson's up in pulpit
an' he d' bummle-on
bout things as I cain't unnerstand
an' volks as deid — an' gone —
'owever *shart* 'is sarmon be —
to me, 'tis tarblish *long!*
   But Ellen Sims d' zet like wood
   as if she's year'n zummat good
   An' bides-on still — when we'm all stood!

An' when 'tis all got awver
we 'angs about outzide
whoiles wimmenvolk d' chatter.
And ther' we 'as t' bide
'til they can yarn wi' Squoire's wife,
or Parson comes long-zide!
   But Ellen Sims d' pass between —
   that *quiet* — she bean't 'ardly zeen . . .
   An *some* — dun' even knaw she's *been!*

I THANK THEE LORD

I thank thee Lord
as I was born
a country chap. So's I can see
the Parish as it used to be.
Old Charlie, ploughing-of 'is lands —
where now they scrapes great 'oles — for sand.

I thank thee Lord as I recall
the quiet. An' the larches tall —
the smell like baccy in the ground —
an' midges, dancin' up-and-down.
An' in the shade, high-up in tree —
the gold-crest, as did say, "Tzee . . . tzee . . ."
Any by the footpath, where't do say
as folk like we must keep away —
the plovers. And the linnets, too —
an' cows as used to graze all through . . .
Oh Lord, 'tis kind
that country chaps like me can mind
the stiles, the hedgerows, an' the meads —
where now there's ballast-heaps, an' weeds . . .

I thank thee I can see again
the bramble-hills. The narrow lane —
maple, an' ash, an' oak-tree tall —
where you could 'ear the blackbird call.
An' in the bushes down the vale —
the singin' — of each nightingale.
And down the bottom of the hill —
I thank thee Lord, that I sees still
the great old elm-tree, stretched so high
that he did seem to sweep the sky!
And shade — led black upon the ground.
I *grieved* lord, when they took he down
so's — where the Carter once led Flower —
we can do seventy mile an hour.

I thank thee I remembers yet
the thickset, and the Jenny's nest
all cool an' hidden in the green.
The vergeside flowers. Thank God I've seen
all these — afore the summer come
and — though they knowed they shouldn't ha' done —
fools fired the straw led on the ground
and scorched the hedges all around.

I thank thee, for when I was boy
how Jim, an' Jes, an' Charl, an' I
did know the Lake from here to yon.
Wild goose — and duck — an' coot — an' swan —

I THANK 'E LARD

I thank 'e Lard
as I was barn
a country chap. Swo's I can zee
the Parish as it used to be.
Owd Charl', ploughin' ov 'is lands —
where now they scraapes gert wholes — vor zand.

I thank 'e Lard as I recall
the quiet, an' the larches tall —
the smell like baccy in the ground —
an' midges, dancen up-and-down.
An' in the sheade, high-up in tree —
the gwold-crest, as did zaay, "Tzee . . . tzee . . ."
Any by the footpath, where 't d' zay
as volk like we must kip awaay —
the plovers. An' the linnets, too —
an' cows as used t' graaze all through . . .
Oh Lard, 'tis kind
as country chaps like me can mind
the stiles, the hedgerows, an' the meads —
where now there's ballast-heaps, an' weeds . . .

I thank 'e I can zee agean
the bramble-hills. The narrow leane —
maple, an' ash, an' oak-tree tall —
where you could yeere the blackbird call.
An' in the bushes down the vale —
the zingen ov each nightingale.
And down the bottom o' the hill —
I thank 'e Lard, that I seez still
the gert wold hellum, streitched swo high
that 'e did zeem to *sweep* the sky!
Wi' sheade — led black upon the ground!
I *grieved* lard, when they took he down
swo's — where the Carter once led Flower —
we can do seventy moile an hour.

I thank 'e I remembers yet
the thickset, an' the Jinny's nest
all cool an' hidden in the green.
The verge-zide vlowers. Thank God I've zeen
all these — avore the summer come
and — though they *knaws* they shouldn't ha' done —
fools voired the straw led on the ground
and scarched the heidges all around . . .

I thank 'e vor when I were bwoy,
'ow Jim, an' Jes, an' Charl, an' I
did knaw the Lake vrom yere to yon.
Wild goose — and duck — an' coot — an' swan —

Jack Heron tryin' to be a reed
wi' bill up-pointed. I thank thee
for pic-nics, swimmin', all the fun
we'ad. Afore the stranger come
and put great fences all about
to keep us village people out.
They says they *shoots* them birds we knew . . .
Oh Lord — I 'opes *they* thanks thee, too!

And — where the turnpike used to be —
I thank thee Lord that folks like me
can call to mind the pony-traps.
Steam-engines — an' the farmers' carts —
tall bicycles, and them as walked
a-carryin' the things they'd bought,
from town to 'ere on Saturdays . . .

Thank-'ee I minds them bygone ways . . .

But now, oh Lord, I must thank thee
for all the motor-cars there be!
For verge cut back, an' road all wide —
an' lay-byes carved-out at the side —
an' juggernauts! Lord — I'll allow
the turnpike gives no pleasure now!
No gossip now! You dare not stay
to talk — nor pass the time o' day!

I thank thee Lord
as I was born
a country chap. So's I can see
the Parish — as it *used* to be!
Old Charlie, ploughin'-of 'is lands —
where now they scrapes great *holes* . . . for *sand* . . . !

Jack Heron tryin' to be a reed
wi' bill up-pwointed. I thank thee
vor pic-nics, swimmen, all the fun
we'ad. Avore the stranger come
an' put gert fences all about
t' keep us village people out.
They says they *shoots* them birds we knew . . .
Oh Lard — I whopes *they* thanks thee, too!

And — where the turnpike used to be —
I thank 'e Lard, as volks like me
d' mind the grit, the pony-traps.
Steam-injines, an' the varmers' carts —
tall bicycles, and them as walked
a-carryen' the things they'd bought,
vrom town to yer on Saturdays . . .

Thank-'e I minds them bygone ways . . .

Nut now, oh Lard, I must thank thee
vor all the motor-cars there be!
Vor verge cut back, an' road all wide —
an' lay-byes carved-out at th' zide —
an' juggernauts! Lard — I'll 'low
the turnpike gies no pleasure now!
Nwo gossip now! Thee dassn't dare stay
t' talk — *nit* pass the time o' day!

I thank 'e Lard
as I was barn
a country chap. Swo's I c'n zee
the Parish — as it *used* t' be!
Old Charl, ploughen' ov 'is lands —
where now they scrapes gert *'oles* . . . vor *zand* . . . !

WORK

YOU'D LIKE TO THATCH YOUR ROOF, SIR?

You'd like to thatch your *roof,* Sir?
  Oh ah! Well let me see . . .
They chimley-pots is *awkward!*
  And *dormers* — h'm! There's three . . .
an eyelet, an' two valleys —
  an' the 'lectric runnin' by —
It won't be all that *easy,* Sir —
  but you might *'ave* a try!

You wants to watch your *straw,* Sir!
  Don't buy it if 'tis *old!*
Ricked bundles can be any age —
  but *hellums* — so I'm told —
do run five to the bundle.
  But if 'twas *me* — I'd choose
wheat-reed as just been *'arvested* —
  an' 'ave it drawed-in — *loose!*

Don't thee forget to wet it!
  Prepare wi' butts before!
Five 'andfull to the hellum —
  I 'ouldn't do no more!
Eight hellums to the *hod,* look —
  an' when 'e's on thy back —
watch-out 'ow you do carry 'im up —
  or else you'll fall down *flat!*

You wants to watch your *spars,* Sir,
  and soak 'em for a day!
And fix they *ledgers* right, sir,
  else straw 'll blow away!
And when you fix the *ridge-cap* —
  make sure you pegs *well down!*
And sow they eaves in tight, look —
  or else they'll dip to ground!

Now what would you be thinking-of?
  *Long*straw? Or Norfolk Spear?
Wheat reed do seem in fashion —
  'tis mostly done round 'ere.
You'll likely find it *awkward* —
  but there — I s'pose the main —
is ain't what it do *look* like —
  as long as it keeps-out *rain!*

Mind you — *what's* that you said, Sir?
  You really didn't know
'twas all that compli-*cated?*

continued on page 42

YOU'D LIKE TO THATCH YOUR ROOF, ZUR?

You'd like to thatch your *roof,* Zur?
Oh ah! Well let me zee . . .
They chimley-pots is *aukurd!*
An' *dormers* — h'm! There's dree . . .
an eyelet, an' two valleys —
an' the 'lecterc runnen by . . .
It wun't be all that *easy,* Zur —
but you met *'ave* a try!

You wants to watch your *straw,* Zur!
Don't buy en if 'tis *old!*
Ricked bundles can be any age —
but *hellums* — swo 'I'm told —
d' run five to the bundle.
But if 'twas *me* — I'd choose
wheat-reed as jus ben *'arvested*
an' 'ave un drawed-in — *loose!*

Dun' thee ferget to wet un!
Wad-up wi' butts avore!
Five 'andful to the hellum —
I shouldn't do n' more!
Eight hellums to the *'od* luk —
an' when 'e's on thee back —
watch-out 'ow you do carr' en up —
or else thee's vall down *flat!*

You wants to watch your *spars,* Zur,
an' soak 'em vor a daay!
An' fix they *ledgers* right, Zur —
else straw 'll blaw awaay!
An' when you does the *ridge-cap* —
meake sure you pags *well down!*
An' zew they eaves in tight, luk —
or else they'll dip t' ground!

Now what would you be a-thinken-ov?
*Long*straw? Or Norfolk spear?
Wheat-reed d' zeem in fashion —
'Tis mostly done round yere.
You'm like t' vind en *aukerd* —
but there — I s'pose the main
is ain't what it d' *luk* like —
as long as't keeps-out *rain!*

Mind you — *wha's* that you zed, Zur?
You really didn't *knaw*
'twere all that there com*pell*icate?

continued on page 43

ROMSEY ABBEY

Dusk is to darkness deep'd. The briar
sunken in shadow, snatches sly
with clawed and unseen hands. The trees
look westward, all in sunset steep'd —
or stand upon the valley's rim
like etchings — on a still, pink sea.
High, high above — a pendant cloud
with brilliant face, looks on the sun.
Stars burn. Fields and the river fade
beneath half-colours, and half-shapes
purple and mauve. Closeby — the sheep
with blank and speechless faces, stare.
And plaintive plovers close to ground
cry warning — of the white owl's wraith.
The Abbey roof yet gleams. The hour
comes stealing from the tower's bulk
past roofs — where swifts which scythe the mists
make wild reply. On into ancient streets
and drowsing gardens, where Night spreads
his mat to sleep. Through windows, walls,
and into homes. So it has been
a thousand years. That all who hear
may say

"Be still. God is."

Opposite: Romsey Abbey
(Photograph: Dick Amey)

Oh — you could *'ave* a go!
— Ah well! We'll 'ave to *see,* Sir
if you'm leavin' it to *me!*
They chimley-pots *is* awkward!
Well now then — let me see . . .

I'll go and tell old *Charlie*
as you do want it done!
Mind you — 'e's *terrible* busy —
I don't know if 'e'll come!
But if 'e do — *we'll* fix it!
We'll make it look real *nice!*
Oh — *we* shall keep the rain out, Sir!
Don't fret about the *price!*

UP BESIDE THE PIG-PENS

Up beside the pig-pens
old Amos, he do plod,
with 'is 'arrows, an' 'is 'orses —
an' a face as looks like God!
Wi' 'is whiskers an' 'is eyebrows
an' 'is dew-drop all a-gleam —
an' 'is beard all streaked an' golden
where 'e *spits* — 'is nicotine!

Down beside the pig-pens
old Amos he do come —
the mare do toss 'er 'ead in *shame*
to 'ear the *language* run —
from that beard as looks like Moses's —
"Come-up — you awkward sod!"
— From them brows as keeps a-wagglin' —
an' that *face* — as looks like *God!*

Aw — you could *'ave* a gwo . . .
Ah well! We'll 'ave to *zee,* Zur
if you'm leavin' it to *we!*
They chimbley-pots *is* aukurd!
Well now then — let I zee . . .

I'll gwo an' tell ole *Char'l*
as you do want un done!
Mind you — 'e's *tarr'ble* busy —
I dunno if 'e'll come!
But if 'e do — *we'll* fix un!
We'll meake un luk real *nice!*
Oh — *we* shall keep the rain out, Zur!
Dun't fret about the *price!*

UP BESIDE THE PIG-PENS

Up bezide the pig-pens
owd Amos, 'e d' plod,
wi' 'is 'arrers an' 'is 'orses —
an' a feace as looks like God!
Wi' 'is whiskers an' 'is eyebrows
an' 'is dew-drop all a-gleam —
an' 'is beard all strekked an' gwolden
where 'e *spets* — 'is nicotine!

Down bezide the pig-pens
owd Amos 'e d' come —
the mare d' toss 'er 'eid in *sheame*
t' 'ear the *langwidge* run —
from that beard as luks like Moses's —
"*Coom-up* — you aukurd sod!"
— From them brows as kips a-wagglen —
an' that *feace* — as looks like *God!*

'ERE'S TO THE OLD 'URDLE-MAKER!

'Ere's to the old 'urdle-maker
an' the coat that 'e got on,
all made by 'imself from a sheepskin —
an' 'ere's to the 'azel-wand!
An' 'ere's to 'e as can do the job
wi' no rod nor twist wound wrong!

'Ere's to the well-made three-foot —
bowed right an' bumped-down true —
an' 'ere's to the heel as won't fall off —
and a weave you cain't *see* through!
An' 'ere's to the twists on the end-sale edge —
not less than ten-and-two!

'Ere's to the man as *knows* 'em —
an' can judge 'em with 'is eye!
Who wants 'em *square* — from top to foot —
who lifts one end to try —
and if they bends an' twists about —
an' won't stay *stiff,* — don't buy!

An' 'ere's to he who cuts the wands —
which is the proper things, —
when they'm *tough* — and *dry* — in the *winter!*
An' when sap do rise in spring —
'ere's to he as won't make 'em *green* —
nor try to sell such a thing!

'Ere's to the man as can *fence* 'em —
and knows, to make 'em last,
they mustn't be rubbed nor chaffed by wind.
So he do fix 'em fast
to *oaken* posts as never rots —
and not that old stub-ash!

So 'ere's to the old 'urdle maker
an' the coat that 'e got on,
all made by 'imself from a sheepskin —
an' ere's to the 'azel-wand!
An' 'ere to 'e as can do the job —
wi' no rod nor twist wound wrong!

YERE'S T' THE OLD 'URDLE-BUMPER!

Yere's t' the old 'urdle-bumper
an' the cwoat that 'e got on,
all cut by 'isself vrom a sheep-skin –
an' yere's t' the 'azel-wand!
An' yere's to 'e as c'n do the job
wi' nar rod nor twist wound wrong!

Yere's to the geate done likely –
well-bowed an' bumped-down true –
an' yere's t' the heel as wun't vall off –
and a wove ye cain't *zee* through!
An' yere's to the twists on the ensale edge –
not less than ten-an'-two!

Yere's t' the man as d' *know* 'em –
an' can *tell* 'em – wi' 'is eye!
Who wants 'em *square* – vrom top t' voot –
who lifts one end t' try –
an' if they bends an' whips about
an' wun't bide *stiff,* – dun't buy!

An' yere's to 'e as coppices 'em –
which is the proper thing –
when wand be *tough* – in *winter!*
An' when sap d' rise in Spring –
Yere's to 'e as doan't meake 'em *green* –
n'r try to *sell* such a thing!

Yere's to the man as zets 'em up!
Who knaws, t' meake 'em last –
the wind mun't be chaff n'r rub 'em.
Swo 'e d' fix 'em fast
wi' *oaken* pwosts as never rots –
an' not that wold stub-ash!

So yere's t' the old 'urdle-bumper
an' the cwoat that 'e got on –
all made by 'isself vrom a sheep-skin –
an' yere's to the 'azel-wand!
An' yere's to 'e as c'n do the job –
wi' nar rod nor twist wound *wrong!*

NEIL THE PLOUGHMAN

Yes, Sir — I'm Neil the Ploughman!
You should ha heard o' me —
for I ploughs from Devon to Yorkshire
as well as 'ere at Leigh —
an' I ploughs from Kent to Oxford —
down to Wales an' back agen —
so's foreigners knows 't'aint easy
for to best the 'Ampshiremen!

Ah — when the 'arvest's done look,
an' finished, come the fall —
I be thinkin' of my plough look —
an' I *swears* I 'ears un call
for to set un, an' to tackle un'
an' to make it balance true —
for the plough do draw old Neil, Sir,
like the 'ounds d' call at *you!*

There's nothin' like a *Ploughin'-Match!*
There's Frank, and Bill, an' Ben —
an' nigh-on anywhere I goes
they'm gathered there *again!*
A-waitin' on the strike-out,
an' the farmers there an' all —
an' the Judge to give the signal
for to tell us we can GO!

I like a bit of *Whole-Work* —
if the furrows nicely pack!
I ain't too bad at *General* —
where you 'as to throw 'em flat!
But *Diggin'* I don't take to —
that there 'roughin'-up the ground' —
nor they new ploughs as always casts
the same way — up or down!

But *High Cut* — that's the *art,* Sir,
an' a pleasure to be seen!
With the furrows well set-up look,
an 'V'd *even* to the seams —
where — old Neil can mind the time, Sir —
they trod in days gone by
on the High Cut, for to hand-cast —
an' 'twas there the *oats* did lie!

Aye — 'twas High-Cut for the oats, Sir —
wi' veerin's straight an' shut
on a clean an' proper job, Sir,

NEIL THE PLOUGHMAN

Yes, Sir — I'm Neil the Ploughman!
  You should ha' heard o' me —
vor I ploughs vrom Devon to Yorkshire
  as well as yere at Leigh —
an' I ploughs vrom Kent to Oxford —
  down to Wales an' back agean —
swo's vurriner knaws 't'aint easy
  vor t' best the 'Ampshiremen!

Ah — when the 'arvest's done luk,
  an' vinished, come the vall —
I be thinken of my plough luk —
an' I *swears* I yeres un call
vor t' zet un an' t' tackle un
  an' meake un balance true —
vor the plough d' draw old Neil, Sir
  Like the 'ounds d' call at *you!*

There's nuthen like a *Ploughen'-Match!*
  There's Frank, and Bill, an' Ben —
an' nigh-on anywheres I gwoes
  they'm gathered ther' *agean!*
A-waitin' on the strike-out —
  an' the varmers there an' all —
wi' the Judge t' give the signal
  vor to tell us we c'n GWO!

I likes a bit o' *'Whole-Work'* —
if the *vors* d' nicely pack!
I ain't too bad at *'General'*
  where you 'as t' throw 'em flat!
But *'Diggen'* I ain't took on —
  that ther' 'roughin-up' the ground —
nit them new ploughs as always casts
  the seame waay up or down!

But *'Igh-Cut'* — that's the *hart,* Sir,
  an' a pleasure t' be zid!
Wi' vors all well set-up luk
  an 'V'd *even* t' the skid —
where — old Neil can mind the time, Sir —
  they trod in days gone by
on the Igh-Cut, vor the 'and-cast —
  and 'twas there the *wutts* did lie!

Aye — 'twas High-Cut vor the wutts, Sir —
  wi' veer'ns straight an' shut
on a clean an' proper job, Sir,

wi' no trace o' weed nor muck —
an' a crest that weren't a rampart —
nor a badly-finished 'grip' —
you *dared not* dig a 'celery-trench' —
or else that *would* be it!

So we do bide at plough look —
an' the gulls do follow-on.
An' we keeps a-going' steady
when the bystanders is gone.
Sometimes it's powerful *cold,* Sir.
an' the frost do bite yer 'ands!
So if folk do cut-off *smartish* — well
the Ploughman understands!

So in they goes to farm-'ouse
an' 'ere alone we stay
wi' a sandwich an' a flask, look —
an' we ploughs an' ploughs away!
But I wish you'd tell your friends, Sir,
to 'urry-up an' come —
if the weather's a bit 'caddly' —
just afore the ploughin's *done!*

For 'tis powerful miserable waitin' —
an' it goes down powerful *bad* —
when the Judge do start by sayin'
what a lovely *meal* 'e's 'ad!
But — takin' good wi bad, look,
'tis *nice* if 'e can say —
"Well — I makes old *Neil the Ploughman*
High-Cut Champion — for the day!"

And should you chance to call, Sir,
in the *beer-tent* later on —
you'll 'ear what they as lost done right —
and they as *won* — done *wrong!*
An' when the fun get goin'
an' wi' smoke the tent turns blue —
you'll see some 'High-Cut' champions, Sir —
an 'Igh-Cut' *judges* — too!

So now you knows the *Plough-lads,* Sir!
Frank, Bill an' Ben an' me —
as ploughs from Devon to Yorkshire
as well as 'ere at Leigh —
as ploughs from Kent to Oxford,
down to Wales an' back again —
so's foreigner knows 't'aint *easy*
for to best the *'Ampshire men!*

Wi' nar trace o' weed or muck —
an' a crest as weren't a rampart —
nor a badly-finished grip —
thee *dassn't* carve nwo 'celery-trench' —
or else that *would* be it!

Swo we d' bide at plough luk —
an' the gulls d' volley-on.
An' we kips a-gwine steady
when the bystanders is gone.
Vor betimes 'tis powerful *cold,* Sir.
an' the frost d' bite yer 'ands!
Swo if volk d' cut-off *smartish* — well
the Ploughman unnerstands!

Swo in they gwoes t' varm-'ouse,
an' yere alone we stay
wi' a sandwich an' a flask luk —
an' we ploughs an' ploughs awaay!
But I wish you'd tell your friends, Sir,
to 'urry-up an' come —
if the weather's a bit caddly —
jus' avore the ploughen's *done!*

Vor 'tis powerful miserable waitin' —
an' it gwoes down powerful *bad* —
when the Judge d' start by sayen'
what a lovely *meal* 'e's 'ad!
But — teaken' good wi bad, luk,
'Tis *nice* if 'e can zay
"Waal — I makes old *Neil the Ploughman*
High-Cut Champion vor the day!"

And should you chance t' call, Sir,
in the *beer-tent* later on —
You'll 'ear what them as lost done right —
an' them as *won* — done *wrong!*
An' when the fun get gwine
an' wi' smoake the tent turns blue —
you'll see some "Igh-Cut' champions, Sir —
an "Igh-Cut' *judges* — too!

Swo now you've met the *Plough-lads,* Sir!
Frank, Bill an' Ben an' me —
as ploughs vrom Devon to Yorkshire
as well as yere at Leigh —
as ploughs vrom Kent to Oxford,
down to Wales an' back agean —
swo's vurriner knaws 't'aint *easy*
vor to best the *'Ampshire men!*

ART

THE EVIL EYE

Who'se squat-down in they beeches yon?
Oh -'e? That feller — Painter John!
I reckon 'e got an *Evil Eye* —
as sees what you nor me can't spy!

I've seen 'im up there on the Down —
paintin' that cromlech — on the crown!
But 'stead o' blackthorns as grows nigh —
he did draw *skeletons* — in the sky!

I've seen 'im by the lytch-gate there!
'Is tombstones — they did stand an' stare!
'Is *tower* — 'ad yellow face - for clock! —
wi' *gargoyles* leered-down from the top!

An' unnerneath the yew-tree's maw —
by belfry stair, an' porch doors tall —
there — standing *quiet* — at the back —
somethin' *unearthly* — dressed in *black!*

I seen 'im in the copse at night —
wi' board an' lantern — after light!
I says, "Watch-out as you don't see no *spook!*"
"I often do!" says 'e. "Jus' look!"

An' down-along through shadows deep —
where owls did bide, an' ghosts did peep —
along the ride, at steady pace —
a *monk* did come — *wi'out a face!*

I s'pose 'tis accordin' to the taste —
if *you* likes folk — without a face!
But I reckon that artist — Painter John —
as squats-down in they beeches yon —

an' wanders round the wood at night —
wi' trees all smudged — an' moon all bright —
do see what you nor me cain't spy —
because 'e've got — the *Hevil Eye!*

THE HEVIL EYE

Who'se scoopied in they beeches yon?
Oh — 'e? Thic veller — Painter John!
Hi reckon 'e've got — a *hevil eye* —
as zeez what thee n'r me cain't spy!

I've a-zeed en up ther' on the Down —
likenen' thic cromlech — on the crown.
But — 'stead o' *blackthorns* as grows nigh —
'e did draw *skellingtons* — in the sky!

Hi zid en up b' lytch-gate there!
'Is tombstawnes — they did stand an' stare!
'Is *tower* — 'ad yaller feace for clock —
wi' *gargoyles* — leeren' down vrom top!

An' unnerneath the yew-tree's maw —
b' belfry stair, an' porch-doors tall —
standin' ther' *quiet* — at the back —
zummat *unearthly* — dressed in *black!*

I zid un in the copse at night
wi' board an' lantern — arter light!
I sez, "Watch-out as you dun't zee nar spook!"
"I often *do!*" sez 'e. "Jes' *look!*"

An' down along through shadows deep —
where owls did bide, an' ghosts did peep —
along the ride at steady peace —
a *monk* did come — *wi'out nar feace!*

I s'pose 'tis 'carden t' the teaste —
if *you* likes volks — as got nar feace!
But I reckons thic artist, Painter John —
as scoopies in they beeches yon —

an' mooches round the woods at night —
wi' trees all smudged, an' moon all bright —
d' zee what thee nor me cain't spy —
because 'e got — the *Hevil Eye!*

GARDENING

PRAYER FOR RAIN

1. Before Rain.

My garden's all baked-up again!
Dear Lord — 'tis time to send-down rain!
My turnips — pepper-'oled by fleas!
Lord — whilt Thou send some *rain* down, please?
My bean-drills lie wi' not a chimp!
They'm gone down t'other way — I thinks!
And where they jiggerin' finches been —
us won't see not a *bit* o' green!
I cain't chase thirsty birds away —
but Lord! 'Tis time for *rain* — I say!

2. After Rain.

A feller cain't 'elp but feel vexed
when you — dear Lord — wi' all respects —
do send-down rain as never stops!
That *'inders* — that don't *'elp'* 'is crops!
No bit o' use is it to chimp-up seed —
and then to smother 'em in weed!
A man can't plant, nor dig, nor 'oe
in ground all turned to *mud,* thee's know!
I'm sorry Lord — but *dang* the rain!
'Ere — wilt Thou shut it *off* again?

THE 'OGWEED BY THE GATE

'Tis the 'ogweed by the gate . . .
He've a-growed up that 'igh
'e is the village wonder
to every passer-by!
But my old Aunt don't *like* it!
She do say "What a *state!*
Whatever 'ave we *comed* to —
wi' *'ogweed* — by the *gate!"*

'Tis the *path* — down to the garden . . .
You've never seen the like!
Beggared if *I* can find it!
Do it wind *left?* Or *right?*
"You cain't get nothing *done!"* she says —
"If you're *old* — or in poor 'ealth!"
H'm . . .
I'll 'ave t' do *some*-thing!
I cain't get through — meself!

PRAYER FOR RAIN

1. Avore rain:

My garden's all baaked-up agean!
Dear Lard — 'tis toime t' zend-down rain!
My tarmut's pepper-wholed b' fleas!
Lard — do 'e zend some *rain* down, please?
My bean-drills lie wi' nar a chimp —
they'm gone down t'other waay, I thinks!
An' where they juggern' finches been —
us wun't zee nar a *bit* o' green!
I cain't chease thirsty birds awaay —
but Lard! 'Tis toime vor *rain* — I d' zay!

2. Arter rain:

A veller cain't 'elp but feel vexed
when you, dear Lard, wi' all respec's —
s' zend-down rain as *never stops!*
That *'inders* — that dun't *'elp'* 'is crops!
Nar bit o' use is 't t' chimp-up zeed —
an' then to smother 'em — wi' weed!
A man cain't plant, nor dig, nor 'oe
in ground all turned to *mud,* thee's knaw!
I'm sorry Lard — but *dang* the rain!
Yere — will 'e shut en *off* agean?

THE 'OGWEED B' THE GEATE!

'Tis the *'ogweed* b' the geate . . .
He've a-grawed up that 'igh —
'e is the village wunner
to every passer-by!
But my old Aunt dun't *like* en!
She d' zay "What a *steate!*
Whatever be we *comed* to —
wi' *'ogweed* — by the *geate!"*

'Tis the *path* as gwoes down garden . . .
You've never zid the loike!
Beggared if *I* c'n vind en!
Do 'er woind *left?* Or *roight?*
"You cain't get nuthen *done!"* she sez —
"If you'm *old* — an' in pore 'ealth!"
H'm . . .
I'll shall ha' t' do *zummat* —
I cain't get through — meself!

'Tis the *smell* comes off the *cooker* . . .
You'd think she would 'ave *said!*
"'Ow *can* I — if you don't come nigh?
You'll find me *gassed* — in *bed* . . .!"
H'm . . .
It *do* pong a bit!
I'd better 'ave a look!
"Not 'til I've finished *breakfast!*
I don't want toast — wi' soot!"

'Tis the drip comes in the green-'ouse . . .
God love us! Fancy *that!*
"I told you near a *month* ago!"
She *did?* Oh yes . . . that *crack!*
H'm . . .
"I'll have to get some putty —
can't do it while 'tis *wet!*
Why not? Well — if 'tis *wet,* my dear —
the bloomin' stuff won't set!"

'Tis the *leaves* — all in the porchway . . .
"Well what shall I do wi' *they?"*
"You *brush 'em up!* 'Cause *I* can't —
an' cart 'em out-the-way!"
"I'll 'ave a *go* at it, my dear!"
"Daresay you *will* — but *when?"*
H'm . . .
Better do it *now* I s'pose —
or I'll never hear the end!

"You ain't been *near* the Churchyard!"
"Who told you *that* — my gel?"
"The Vicar! Maud's grave's a *disgrace!*
And *Grandma's* is — as *well!"*
H'm . . .
Whenever do it *finish* —
this 'You-ain't-done-it' song?
They sings it all the time they'm *'ere* —
they don't *stop* — when they'm *gone!*

'Tis the *stink* comes off the *cooker* . . .
You'd think she 'ould 'a *zed!*
"'Ow *can* I — if you dun't come nigh?
You'll vind me *gassed* — in *bed!*"
H'm . . .
'E *do* pong a bit —
I'd better 'ave a luk!
"Not 'til I've finished *breakfast!*
I dun' want toast — wi' soot!"

'Tis the *drip* comes in the *green-*'ouse . . .
Cawd lumme! Fancy *that!*
"I *twold* 'e near a *month* agwo!"
'Er *did?* Oh ah . . . that *crack!*
H'm . . .
"I'll ha' t' git some putty —
Cain't do it whoiles 'tis *wet!*
Wny *not?* Well — 'lest 'tis *dry,* my dear —
the blimmen stuff wun't zet!"

'Tis the *leaves* — all in the porchway . . .
"Waal what shall I do wi' *they?*"
"You *brush 'em up!* 'Cause *I* cain't —
An' cart 'em out-the-way!"
"I'll 'ave a *gwo* at 'em my dear!"
"Dessay you *will* — but *when?*"
H'm . . .
Better do it *now* I s'pose —
or I'll never 'ear the end!

"You ain't been *near* the Churchyard!"
"Who told 'e *that* — my gel?"
"The Vicar! Maud's grave's a *disgrace!*
And *Grandma's* is — as *well!*"
H'm . . .
Whenever do it *finish* —
this 'You-ain't-done-it' zong?
They zings it all the time they'm *yer* —
they dun't *stop* — when they'm *gone!*

WHO LIVES IN FARMER TOM'S OLD HOUSE?

Who lives in *Farmer Tom's* old house?

Cain't say as I know *he* . . .
The gate be shut. The door be closed.
I seen a man go down the road —
'e never spoke to *me!*

Who lives in Bunney's *cottages?*

Cain't say as I know *they!*
I put me 'and up once — in lane . . .
Cain't say I ever will again . . .
They 'adn't aught t' say . . . !

What o' they *new* folk — up the hill?

They bain't so bad, I'll allow!
They seemed to sort-of *want* to speak —
the girl *smiled* once — in Lower Street.
She *generally* chatters, now!

Well — things *do* change . . .

Ah! 'Tain't that long
as *Tom* leaned on that gate . . .
"Hyup — I seen thee down-along!"
'e'd holler. "How y' goin'-on?"
"Aw — fair-to-middlin' mate!

And can you mind — at Bunney's place —
the children all at play?
The pigsties? And the timber-stack?
The fowls in fowl-run at the back?
It's not like *that — today* . . .
All *strangers* . . .

Well — us can't 'elp that!

Us *can't!* I *knows!* But still . . .
There's only thee and me left now . . .
P'raps 'alf-a-dozen more, I allow . . .

Then — who'se the *strangers,* Bill . . . ?

WHO LIVES IN FARMER TOM'S OLD HOUSE?

Who lives in *Farmer Tom's* old house?

Cain't zay as I knows *he* . . .
The geate be shut. The door be closed.
I zid a man gwo down the road —
'e never spwoke to *me!*

Who lives in Bunney's *cottages?*

Dunno as I knaws *they!*
I put me 'and up oncest — in leane . . .
Dunno as I ever 'ull agean . . .
They 'adn't aught t' zay . . . !

What o' they *new* folk — up the hill?

They bean't swo bad, I'll low!
Zome zeems t' sart o' *want* t' speak —
the gal *smoiled* oncest — in Lower Street.
She *gen'lly* chatters, now!

Waal — things *do* cheange . . .

Ah! 'Tain't that long
as *Tom* leaned on thic geate . . .
"Hyup! I zid thee down-along!"
'e'd 'oller. "'Ow bis't gwine on?"
"Aw — vair-t'-middlen, mate!

An' do 'e mind, at Bunney's pleace —
the chillern all at plaay?
They pigsties? That 'ere timber-stack?
They vowls in vowl-run at the back?
Tain't much like *that* — *todaay* . . .
All *strangers* . . .

Waal — us cain't odds that!

We *cain't!* I *knaws!* But still . . .
there's on'y thee and me left now . . .
P'raps 'alf-a-dozen more, I'll 'low . . .

Then — who'se the *strangers,* Bill . . . ?

LOOKING BACK

LET'S GO UP TO TROAKS, JIM

Let's go up to Troaks, Jim!
Let's wander-on up lane . . .
I'd like t' see the Elm Grove
an' The Rookery again . . .

They great old elms is *felled,* Dad!
There's nothin' there to *see* . . .
The rooks is gone — the hedges down —
the land all *open* be!

Well — let's go up to Picket-piece!
Through Narley's — an' Preez Day —
then carry-on up round Bellropes —
and come back round Payne's Hey!

I'd *like* t' see they fields again —
where we was all young chaps
a-singin' in the hoeing-gangs —
from Scoots to Pitts — and back!

Well — things 'ave all been *altered,* Dad!
It ain't the *same* today!
The Maple-run — an' Kettle Bank —
they all been took *away!*

'Tis *all* — one great long fallow
far as the eye can see!
Wi' just *one chap* to work it all —
it wouldn't interest *thee!*

Well — we could go by *Puckeridge's* . . .
I knows they bain't there *now!*
But the new folks as 've comed there
cain't change it *much* — I'll 'low!

There bain't no 'new folks' *there,* Dad!
The house bides dark, an' still —
sat *empty*-like — an *quiet* —
like *death* — upon the hill!

You'll ha' to *understand,* Dad —
how *altered* 'tis today!
They farm roads and they meads you knew —
they all been *took away!*

LET'S GWO UP TO TROAKS, JIM!

Let's gwo up to Troaks, Jim!
Let's twober-on up leane . . .
I minds t' zee the Elm Grove
an' The Rookery agean . . .

They gert wold elms is *felled,* Dad!
There's nothen ther' t' *zee . . .*
The rooks is gone — the heidges down —
the land all *awpen* be!

Well — let's gwo up t' Picket-Piece!
Through Naarley's — an' Preez Day —
then carr' on up roun' Bell Ropes —
an' come back roun' Payne's Hey!

I'd *like* t' zee they fields agean —
where we was all bwoy-chaps —
a-zingen' in the hoein' gangs —
vrom Scoots t' Pitts an' back!

Waal — things is all ben *altered,* Dad!
It bean't the *zeame* t'daay!
The Maple-run — an' Kittle Bank —
they all ben took *awaay!*

'Tis all one gert long valler
far as the eye c'n zee!
Wi' jes *one chap* t' work it all —
it 'ouldn't interest *thee!*

Waal — we c'd gwo by *Puckeridge's . . .*
I knaws they bean't there' *now!*
But the new folks as 've comed ther'
'un't cheanged en much — I'll 'low!

There bean't no new folks *there,* Dad!
The house bides dark, an' still —
set empty-like, an' quiet —
like *death* — stood on the hill!

Thee's 'll ha' t' *unnerstand,* Dad,
how *altered* 'tis todaay!
They farm roads an' they meads you knew —
they all ben took *awaay!*

The Puckeridges, the Blundells,
the Pitts an' Wallingtons —
and all them places round about —
they'm *swallered-up!* And *gone!*

And all the land is fallen
to folks as don't *know* we!
Like sportin' gents from London —
as you might *never* see!

Ah well — I s'pose you *knows,* Jim!
I've a bit *'ere* t' do . . .
Daresay I can *amuse* meself
without a-troublin' you . . .

But there — 'twas just a *thought,* Jim —
the weather bein' fine!
I'll poke-about in *garden* . . .
We'll go — some *other* time!

EVENING

WHEN SUN DO DIP

When sun d' dip
be'ind Church Spire —
it sort o' sets
the *thatch* a-fire!
And down by mead
half gold, half green —
the elms do stand
and *watch!*
It d' seem
the birds all up
an' home from ground
is *arguin'*
all up-an'-down —
in hedge, in copse
afore the sun —
so's you cain't speak
for *hark*enun'!
An' rooks as broad
as 'Ampshirmen
do swear an' *holler* —
up the lane —
when sun d' dip
be'ind Church Spire —
an' sort o' sets
the *thatch* a-fire.

The Puckridge's, the Blundells,
the Pitts an' Wallingtons —
an all them pleaces round about —
they'm *swallered-up!* An' *gone!*

An' all the land is vallen
t' volks as dun't *knaw* we!
Like sportin' gents vrom Lunnon —
as you met *never* zee!

Ah well — I s'pose you *knaws,* Jim!
I've a bit *yer* t' do . . .
Dessay I c'n *amuse* meself
wi'-out a-troublen you . . .

But there . . . 'twas jes' a *thott,* Jim —
the weather bein' voine!
I'll pwoke about in garden . . .
We'll gwo — some *other* toime!

WHEN ZUN D' DIP

When zun d' dip
be'ind Church spoire —
'e zart o' zets
the *thatch* avoire!
An down b' mead
ha'fe gwold, ha'fe green —
the hellums d' stand
an' *watch!*
D' zeem
the birds all up
an' whoam vrom ground
is *argivvyen*
up-an'-down —
in heidge, in copse
avore the sun —
swo's you cain't speak
vor *'arkenun!*

An' rooks as broad
as 'Ampshire-men
d' swear an' *'oller* —
Up the leane —
when zun d' dip
be'ind Church spoire —
an' zart o' zets
the *thatch* avoire.

THE DROWNER

Well I'll be hemmed! I didn't see
the sun go down! Now dew be come
to make the mead as wet can be!
And carrier be creepin' down
wi' mist a-coming off, I see!
And bat-mouse, he do flick and twitter —
whiles duck do follow mate upriver!

I saw *vole* splash! And bubbled cut
across the stream. *Fish* did jump then!
Trees' images lies downside-up —
and by the mist, old cob and pen
lie fast asleep — wi' heads wing-tucked.
Light have gone down to glimmer — so
I can't bide *here!* 'Tis time to go . . .

DIDN'T SEE THE LAPWING?

Dids't see the lapwing running round
a-trailing her poor wing on ground
when sun went down?

Dids't see the flock go dashin' by
all black-and-white up, up in sky?
. . . Dids't hear 'er *cry* . . . ?

Dids't see the owl float up in tree
as cunnin' — an' as *quick* could be?
. . . Dids't *see* . . . ?

Dids't see the lapwing *quiet* go —
and hide in sedge — where brook do flow . . . ?
Dids't see 'er *go* . . . ?

THE DROWNER

Well I'll be hemmed! I didn't zee
the zun gwo down! Now dew be come
t' meake the mead as wet can be!
An' carrier be creepen' down
wi' mist a-comen off, I d' zee!
And bat-mouse he do flick and twitter —
whiles duck d' volley meate up-river.

I zid *vole* splash! An' bubbles cut
athirt the stream. *Fish* did jump then!
Trees' images lie downzid-up —
an' by the mist, wold cob an' pen
lies fast asleep, wi' heids wing-tucked.
Light 'ave gone down to glimmer — swo
I mun't bide *yere.* 'Tis time t' gwo . . .

DIDS'T ZEE THE LAPWING RUNNEN' ROUND?

Dids't see the lapwing runnen round
a-trailen 'er pore wing on ground
when zun went down?

Dids't zee the flock gwo dashen' by
all black-an'-white, up, up in sky?
. . . Dids't year 'er *cry* . . . ?

Dids't zee the owl float up in tree —
as cunnen — an' as *quick* could be?
. . . Dids't zee . . . ?

Dids't zee the lapwing *quiet* gwo —
an' hide in *seidge* — where brook d' flow . . . ?
Dids't zee 'er *gwo* . . . ?

GROWING OLD

WHEN WIND DO BLOW

When wind do blow, an' ash-trees bend —
I thinks as I be *young* again . . . !
I eases-up from mangold-hoein' —
an' *watches* — where the wind be goin' . . .

I see the couch go down in mead —
an' rooks all *bowled-along* like leaves —
an' hedges — *all* a-bounce and shake —
wi' *poplars* — leanin' fit to break!
An' in the copse — when wind tears through —
it *bugles* — like a *bullock,* you . . . !

And fence do twang just like an 'arp . . . !

Then *down* the mead I wants to start
an' *run* wi' wind — an' *shout* wi' joy —
like I did once — when I were boy . . . !

But I must bide — an' keep a-goin' —
an' scrape away — at mangold-hoein' . . .
'Cause I knows I *bain't* young again —
when wind do blow, an' ash-trees bend . . .

I SEE THE YEW-TREE

I see the yew-tree stood here still —
a great old feller on the hill —
wi' dried old heart, an' grey wi' age —
a-castin' of 'is black old shade —
as calls to mind such things as monks
an' ghosts o' folks as walked 'ere once —

I see he bides here — still . . .

I see the great old elms still stands
wi' arms all folded! Like a band
o' grannies gossipin athwart
the brow, wi' children at the skirt.
And whiles they gossips, years do fly.
Boys plays, men works, and old 'uns die —

but *they* bides on here — still . . .

I sees the beeches standin' tall
as princes in a palace hall —

WHEN WIND D' BLAW

When wind d' blaw, an' ash-trees bend —
I thinks as I be *young* agean . . . !
I eases-up vrom mangold-hoen' —
an' *watches* — where the wind be goen . . .

I seez the couch gwo down in mead —
an' rooks all *bowled-along* — like leaves —
an pleaches — *all* a-bounce and sheake —
wi' *poplars* — leanin' fit t' break!
An' in the copse — when wind tears droo —
un *bugles* — like a *bullock,* you . . . !

An' fence d' twang jes' like an 'arp . . . !

Then *down* the mead I wants t' start
an' *run* wi' wind — an' *shout* wi' jiy —
like I did oncest — when I were bwoy . . . !

But I must bide — an' kip a-gwine —
an' scraape awaay — at mangold-hoen' . . .
'Cause I knaws I *bean't* young agean —
when wind d' blaw, an' ash-trees bend . . .

I D' ZEE THE YEW-TREE . . .

I d' zee the yew-tree stood yere still —
a gert wold veller on the hill —
wi' dried wold heart, an' grey wi age —
a casten' ov 'is black wold sheade —
as calls t' mind sech things as monks —
an' gwosts o' volks as walked yere, oncest —

I zee *'e* bides yere, still . . .

I d'zee they gert wold hellums still stands
wi' arms all fwolded! Like a band
O' grannies gossipin' athirt
the brow, wi' chillern-sprigs at skirt
An' whoiles they gossips years d' vly!
Bwoys plays, men works, an' old 'uns die —

but *they* bides on yere, still . . .

I d' zee the beeches stood-up tall
as princes in a palace hall —

a-listenin' as down-along
linnet do sing his minstrel-song!
And leaves as curls when they do fall
by butts, like *parchments* scroll on scroll —

I sees *they* falls here, still . . .

And in the grove, up high above
the hazel-wands — my great old Love —
the Ash-Tree maiden still stands there
with velvet buds all in 'er hair . . .
And do stretch fingers to beseech
the *sun* — to warm-out each green leaf!

I see *she* stands here, still!

And oaks — like sextons — I do see
still holds aloft great gloomy wreathes —
and still like giants in the sky
do lower on them as do pass by!
What do *they* reckon o' lives o' men?
Why-nothing! Depends upon it when

we go — *they'll* be here, still!

Bide then old trees — bide on in peace!
Black yew-tree feller — princely beech —
great elms — an' oaks with years all weighed —
and my old Love — the Ash-Tree maid!
And should one fall to such as we —
let he who takes thee — *kindly* be!

. . . 'Til then — bide *on* here — *still!*

a-*harkenun* — as down-along
linnet d' zing 'is minstrel-song!
An' leaves as curls — when they d' vall
by butts, like *parchments* — scroll on scroll —

I seez *they* valls yere, still . . .

An' in the grawve, up high above
the 'azel-wands — my gert wold Love —
the *Ash-Tree* maiden still stands there
wi' velvet buds all in 'er hair . . .
And d' streitch vingers t' beseech
owd zun — t' warm-out each green leaf!

I see *she* stands yere, still!

An' woaks, like sextons — I d' zee
still hists aloft gert, gloomy wreathes —
an' still like giants in the sky
do lower on them as d' pass by!
What do *they* reck o' lives o' men?
Why nothen! Pend upon it when

we'm gone, *they'll* be yere still!

Bide then wold trees — bide on in peace!
Black yew-tree veller — princely beech —
gert hellums — an woaks wi' years all weighed —
an' my wold Love, the Ash-Tree maid!
An' should arn vall t' sech as we —
let 'e who teakes thee — *kindly* be!

. . . 'Till then — bide *on* yere — *still!*

BILLY'S CHOICE

The old horse days — unhurried ways —
the tall cart by the hedge . . .
and hands held when I should 've been
deliverin' the bread . . .

Walks in the summer countryside —
the soft air — an' the kisses . . .
we cannot *lose* when I did choose
to make of *you* — my *Missis!*

I found it, off the beaten track
easy to live with you.
I liked the good old *country* folk
we got along with, too.

So I must mind the simple things
we *loved.* And — not too sad —
remind myself as I cain't lose —
what we both knows — we've *'ad!*

DYING

MY OLD CHAP

My Old Chap do lie in bed . . .
The wind do swing at curtain. Oh
sun d' shine —
no bird d' sing —
Jesse d' down the turnpike go —
an' my Old Chap lies — *listening* . . .

My Old Chap don't want 'is pipe . . .
He filled it — put it down. Oh
he don't *talk*
about such thing —
nor *fuss* — because 'e got to go . . .
'E just do *bide* there — *listening* . . .

My Old Chap do lie in bed.
Curtain do 'ang down *still.* Oh
sun d' shine —
no bird d' sing —
the thatch d' keep 'im cool. So
he d' lie there — *listening* . . .

BILLY'S CHOICE

Th' owd hoss-daays, an' quiet waays —
the cart stood b' the heidge . . .
an' wholden' hands when I should ha' ben
deliverin' the bread . . . !

Walks in the zummer countryzide —
the balmy air — the kisses . . .
us cassn't *lose* when I did choose
t' meake o' thee — my *Missus!*

I vound un off the busy track
aizy t' live wi' you.
I liked the good wold *country* volks
we got along wi', too.

Swo I must mind they little things
we *loved.* I mun't be zad . . .
I'll mind myself as I cain't lose —
what we bwoth *knaws* — we've *'ad!*

MY OLD CHAP

My Owd d' lie in bed . . .
The wind d' swing at curtain. Oh
zun d' shoine —
nwo bird d' zing —
Jesse d' down the turnpike gwo —
an' my Owd Chap lies — *lissenin'* . . .

My Owd Chap dun' want 'is pipe . . .
'e villed en. Put en down. Oh
'e dun' *talk*
about sech things —
n'r *fuss* because 'e got t' gwo . . .
'E jes d' *bide* there — *lissenin'* . . .

My Owd Chap d' lie in bed.
Curtain do 'ang down *still.* Oh
zun d' shoine —
nwo bird d' zing —
the thatch d' keep un cool. Swo
'e d' lie there — *lissenin'* . . .

BEREAVEMENT

I DIDN'T KNOW JES HAD PASSED AWAY!

I didn't know Jes 'd passed away!
I only *seen* 'n — yesterday!
God bless us — we shain't 'alf miss he!
Down pub — we shain't know *where* we be!

They songs 'e sung of long ago!
Why — some my old *Dad* didn't know!
Not bellerin' drunk — but full of *fun* —
and *light,* and *bright* — they songs he sung!

Up'd go 'is pot! "I'll give thee a toast!
Here's meat to the Master — *he* takes most!
Fat to the Missus, and to the kids —
soup to the *servants* — scrump to the dids!

"Bones to the dogs, Sirs — *grissle* to the cat —"
I wonder where he go 'old o' *that?*
"And here's to the pint that just been gone —
and to he as brings the *next* one on!"

Cawd — how they townies laughed! And *paid!*
But Jes didn't *beg!* 'Twas just 'is way —
and on the days when *he* was flush —
'twas, "Going t' 'ave one wi' *me* then, Mush?"

'Bout nine, 'e'd say "Well I'll *depart!*
Cause I cain't *see* much — after dark!"
We *laughed!* Old Jes 'ad sharper sight
than *most* — as does their work-at night!

I didn't know Jes 'ad passed away!
I only *saw* 'im yesterday!
Gawd bless us — we shan't 'alf miss he
down *pub!*

We shain't know *where* we be!

I DIDN'T KNAW JES 'D PASSED AWAAY!

I didn't knaw Jes 'd passed awaay!
I on'y *zid* un — yesterday!
Cawd lumme — we shain't 'alf miss *'e!*
Down pub — we shain't knaw *where* we be!

They songs 'e zung ov long-agwo!
Why zome — my old *Dad* din't knaw!
Not beller'n drunk — but vull o' *fun* —
an' *loight,* an' *broight* — they zongs 'e zung!

Up'd gwo 'is pot! "I'll gie thee a *to-ast!*
'ere's meat t' the Maister — 'e teakes moast!
Fat t' the Missus, an' t' the kids —
soup t' the *sarvents* — scrump to the dids!

"Bwoanes t' the dogs, Zurs — grissle t' the cat —"
I wunners where 'e got whold o' *that?*
"An' yeres t' the pint as jes ben gone —
an' to 'e as brings the *next* one on!"

Cawd — 'ow they townies laafed! An' *paaid!*
But Jes didn't beg! 'Twas jest 'is waay —
an' on the days when *'e* was flush —
'twas "Gwine 'ave one wi *me* then, Mush?"

'Bout nine 'e'd say, "Well — I'll *depaart!*
'Cause I cain't *zee* much arter dark!'
We *laafed!* Ole Jes 'ad sharper sight
than *mwoast* — as does their work — at night!

Hi din't knaw Jes 'd passed awaay!
I on'y *zid* un yesterdaay!
Cawd lumme! We shain't 'alf miss 'e
down pub!
We shain't knaw *where* we be!

CHRISTMAS BE COME

Christmas be come.
Weather be *'ard!*
Frost — do hang white in lane.
Woods be all dark —
hedges *stark* —
snow do come back again . . .

Rooks do bide home.
Plover do *cry*.
Cows — be all stood by gate.
House-mouse do scratch —
dusk do come down.
Flames is all *blue* in grate.

Kettle do sing —
tea's been all laid.
Children comes in from play.
Vixen do scream.
Owl sits in tree.
"Whit-*wheet!* Whit-*wheet!*" he d' say.

WHEN CHRISTMAS PASSED THIS WAY

When Christmas passed this way —
we comed up to the Church.
We filled-up all the pews.
We sat, we sung, we prayed . . .
We 'eard again the good old tale —
the Parson, he did say
"A *stable* was his birth-place —
an' 'umble was 'is way . . ."

Then afterwards — 'e shook our 'ands.
And wished us a good day.
Then — 'e got in 'is motor-car —
and' 'e did drive away . . .

When Christmas passed this way —
we comed up to the Pub.
We 'adn't got *over* yesterday.
But still! It wouldn't be right
if we'd missed Frank, and Fred and they —
who'd come back home to see us
from villages away.
We drank — we laughed — we sang.
"Happy Christmas!" we did say
to them we'd pass with not a word
on any *other* day . . .

CHRISTMAS BE COME

Christmas be come.
Weather be *'ard!*
Frost — do 'ang white in leane.
Woods be all dark —
heidges leary —
snaw d' come back agean . . .

Rooks d' bide whoam.
Plover d' *cry.*
Cows — be all stood b' geate.
'Ouse-mouse d' scratch —
dusk d' come down.
Fleames is all *blue* in greate.

Kittle d' zing —
tea ben all laid.
Chillern comes in vrom plaay.
Vixen d' scream.
Owl zets in tree.
"Whit-*wheet!* Whit-*wheet!*" he d' zay.

WHEN CHRISTMAS PASSED THIS WAAY

When Christmas passed this waay —
we comed up to the Church.
We villed-up all the pews.
We zet, we zung, we praayed.
We yeard agean the good wold tale —
the Passon, 'e did zay
"A *stable* was 'is birth-pleace —
an' *'umble* was 'is waay . . ."

Then arterwards — 'e shook our 'ands.
An' wished us a good daay.
Then 'e got in 'is motor-car —
an' 'e did drive awaay . . .

When Christmas passed this waay —
we comed down to the pub.
We 'adn't got *awver* yesterdaay.
But still! 'T 'ouldn't be roight
if we'd missed Frank, an' Fred an' they
as comed back whoam t' zee us
from villages awaay.
We drank — we laffed — we zung.
"'Appy Christmas!" we did zaay
t' they we'd pass wi' nar a word
on any *other* daay . . .

Then — we got in our motor-cars —
and we did drive away . . .

When Christmas passed *this* way —
the youngsters came to town.
They stood-up by the Gents.
And what they 'ad to say
was just the same as what was said
on any *other* day . . .
'Cept — p'raps — they said it *louder!*
For bein' Christmas Day
there were more of 'em to *stare.* And more
of *we* — to stare at *they!*

Then — they got on their motor-bikes —
and they did *roar* away . . .

When Christmas passed *this* way —
it comed that *quiet* — and *still* —
you might 'ave 'ardly *noticed* it!
But Bert, and Auntie May —
were 'ere for Christmas dinner —
and afterwards did stay.
To talk of Dad — and Mother —
Gert and Flo — all passed away . . .
An' 'ow Tory sang the carols
in the years of yesterday . . .

Then — we did *kiss* each other.
"Come more *often!*" we did say!
And they got in *their* motor-car —
an' *they* did drive away . . . "

When Christmas passed this way —
another *Crib* they made!
The same old box — an' wooden cows —
we saw *last* Christmas day!
The same old dollies — starin' stiff —
at where the Babe d' lay!
. . . But — looke-ye at them *children!*
They comes . . . they stares . . . they *stays!*
"There's *sheep* in there — an' *oxen!*
An' there's *Mary!*" one d' say!
"An' there's *Shepherds* look! *An'* Angels!
And *Three Wise Men* — to *pray!*"

They think 'tis *marvellous* — well, you *do* —
when you'm as young as they!
'Twon't hurt t' bide *on* a bit —
afore we drives away . . . !

Then — we got in our motor-cars —
an' we did drive awaay . . .

When Christmas passed *this* waay —
the *bwoy-chaps* comed in town.
They stood up b' the Gents.
An' what they 'ad t' zaay
was 'bout the seame as what was zed
on any *other* daay . . .
'cept — p'raps — they zed it *louder!*
Vor bein' Christmas Daay
there were more on 'em t' *stare.* An more
o' *we* t' stare at *they* . . .

Then — they got on their motor-bikes —
an' they did *roar* awaay . . .

When Christmas passed *this* waay —
it comed that *quiet,* an' *still* —
you met 've 'ardly *nawticed* 't!
But Bert, an' Auntie May —
they comed vor Christmas dinner —
an' arterwards did stay.
T' talk of Dad — an' Mother —
Gert an' Flo — all passed awaay . . .
An' 'ow Tory sang the carols
in the years of yesterdaay . . .

Then — we did *kiss* each other.
"Come more *oft'ner!"* we did zaay!
And they got in *their* motor-car —
an' *they* did drive awaay . . . !

When Christmas passed this waay —
another *Crib* they'd made!
Th' zeam wold box — an wooden cows —
we zid *last* Christmas Daay!
The 'zeame wold dollies starin' stiff —
at where the Babe d' lay!
. . . But — luk 'ee at they *chillern!*
They comes — they stares — they *stays!*
"There's *sheep* in there — an' *oxen!*
An' there's *Mary!"* one d' zay!
"An' there's *Shepherds* luk! An' *Angels!*
An' *Three Wise Men* — t' pray!"

They thinks 'tis *marvellous!* Well — you *do* —
when you'm as young as they . . . !
'Twun't 'urt — t' bide-*on* a bit —
avore we drives awaay . . .

TAILPIECE

Father cut the nettles from the eighteenth century headstone in the old part of the Churchyard. He said,

"Have you seen *this,* boy?"

I could not make-out the name of the occupant of the grave, but I *could* read the legend underneath.

Stay, Friend, and Think,
e'er Thou pass by,
As thou art Now, so Once was I.
As Now I am, so Shalt Thou be.
Prepare Thyself to follow Me!

Father's eyes twinkled.
"Do you know the answer to *that,* boy?"
'No!" I said. "I don't know, Dad! What is it?"
He said:-

"To follow thee — I'm not content —
for none can tell which way th' art went!"

GLOSSARY

ackle	to work, function
agg	egg
agrivvy	argue
arn	any
arter	after
athirt	across
aukurd	awkward
avore	before
bain't	am not
bat-mouse	bat
bean't	am not
betimes	sometimes, now and again.
bide	stay
bist	(be-est thou) Are you?
bummle	to talk or act confusedly
bwoy-chap	young man
caddly	unsettled
carrier	main artificial stream from river to watermeadow
cast	throw
cast	(can'st, can'st thou,) Can.
cassn't	(Can'st not) Cannot
chimp	sprout
chivvey	nag
cob	male swan
compellicate	complicated
coom	come
copse	small wood
coppice	to cut small wood
crest	top edge of ploughed furrow
cwoat	coat
dang	dam
dassn't	(darest not) dare not
deid	dead
diggen'	digging, deep-ploughing
dormer	roof-window
downzid-up	unside-down
dree	three
droo	through
drowner	man who maintains the watermeadows
eave	lower edge of thatched roof
ef	if
ef'n	if
ensale	end'sale' or upright of a hurdle
eyelet	window with top level with the eave

gawp	stare stupidly
geate	gate, or three-foot hurdle
gert	large
green	with sap in
grip	bottom trench as in ploughing
gwine	going
Hand-cast	hand-sowing (corn)
heel	bottom of hurdle
heidge	hedge
hellum	'helm' — straw 'tile' used in thatching
hellum	elm
high-cut	high, sharp ploughing
hoss	horse
janty	jaunty
jiy	joy
jugger	diminutive of swear-word 'bugger'
leate	late
leane	lane
leary	sparse, bare, gaunt, uncomfortably cold
ledger	split hazel-wand pegged across top of thatch
likely	properly, well
low'ren	lowering, threatening
luk	look
lurcher	sagacious poaching-dog, trained to silence
mangold	large fleshy root for cows; of beetroot family
marm	madam
mead	meadow, field
mush	to wander aimlessly to be about for ulterior motive, stealing or poaching 'fellow' — as in fellow-poacher or gypsey
narn	none, not any
nit	nor
'od	hod
pen	female swan
plaze	please
pleach	section of a laid or trimmed hedge
pwoke	poke
quorlsome	quarrelsome
reddled	red, like brick
rick	large stack of hay or corn or straw
ridge-cap	top ridge of thatched roof

skid	furrow-bottom as in ploughing
spar	split thatching-peg
squiggen	peering or squinting
squinney	child crying
storm-cock	mistle-thrush
swo	so
stoop	to swoop, also to settle as bird on eggs
tackle	to set-up
tag	castrated male sheep
tarmut	turnip
thic	this, or that
thic-waays	this way or that way
tutuths	two-toothed
tober	to walk
toby, on the	to be tramping
un	one, also it he, her, him.
vall (the)	autumn
valler	fallow, ploughed land or for ploughing
valley	adjoining slope between two roofs at right-angles to each other, as in thatching.
veer'n	lead-out, as in starting furrow of ploughing
vor	for, also 'furrow'
vust	first
wad	straw heap for thatching
whirren	purring call
whoam	home
whole-work	flat, broken ploughing
wold	old
wook-off	turn right
wove	weave in the hurdle
wutts	oats
yaw	ewe
year	hear
yer, yere	here
zet	sit

SOME PUBLISHED WORK BY NORMAN GOODLAND

Garnett Daubenay's Pipe	Macdonald
Sexton's Boy	Hutchinson
My Father Before Me	Hutchinson
Old Stan's Diary	John Baker
Villages	Mills and Boon
Down on the Farm	Paul Cave
Country Craftiness	Paul Cave
Morning Stories	Paul Cave
Thicways & Athirt	Robert Hale
Radio Country Diary	Paul Cave

Medical Books:-

Coronary Care	John Wright
Intensive Care	John Wright

Contributions to:-

Book of Leisure	Odhams
Woman's Hour 1	BBC Publications
Woman's Hours 2	BBC Publications

Recordings:-

My Old Chap	Saydisc Records
Goodland's Year	BBC Radio Solent
Goodland's People	BBC Radio Solent

ACKNOWLEDGEMENTS

Saydisc Records
Hampshire County Magazine
Southern Printers
Macdonald and Janes Publishers Ltd
Adams and Charles Black Publishers

for their kind permission in allowing the use of poems recorded and published in their journals.